LOVE

LOVE

Valerie Martin

Little Books by Big Names™

First published in the United Kingdom in 2005 by Little Books Ltd,
48 Catherine Place, London SW1E 6HL

10 9 8 7 6 5 4 3 2 1

Text copyright © 2005 by Valerie Martin
Design and layout copyright © 2005 by Little Books Ltd

A CIP catalogue record for this book is available from the British Library.

ISBN: 1 904435 28 9

The author and publisher will be grateful for any information that will assist them
in keeping future editions up-to-date. Although all reasonable care has been taken in the
preparation of this book, neither the publisher, editors nor the author can accept any liability
for any consequences arising from the use thereof, or the information contained therein.

Many thanks to: Jamie Ambrose for editorial production and management,
Debbie Clement and Mousemat Design Limited for jacket and text design,
Craig Campbell of QSP Print for printing consultancy.
Printed and bound by Scotprint in Scotland.

Every attempt has been made by the publishers to trace the copyright holders.
Any omissions will be rectified in future reprints.

CONTENTS

Love   7

Surface Calm   19

Messengers   47

The Mechanics of It   67

Contraction   77

Transposing   97

The Creator Has a Master Plan   119

LOVE

The man I am talking to wants to kill me. He has a knife in his pocket and in the last five minutes he has begun to feel the weight of that knife, just above his groin. He has even gone so far as to trace the outline of the knife inside his pocket with his fingertips, under the table, where I can't see. We have a table between us but it's a small table and he could grab me by my hair and pull me forward easily, turning my body away as he pulled me by the hair so that I would be stretched backward across the table and he could bring the blade down along my throat. There would be a second as the blade slit into my throat when there would be no blood and then, with what satisfaction would he watch the thin line fill with blood, overflow. He would pull my head down a little farther towards him, so that the blood would run over my chin, my face, into my nostrils and over my eyes.

Since it is my eyes that he particularly despises.

He considers another possibility. Why not just take my head between his palms and gouge out the offending eyeballs with his thumbs. He stretches his large hands on the table between us.

My own hands, small, white, useless, busy themselves with a pen. 'Do you have a car?' I inquire.

He doesn't answer. He wants me to ask this question again, to look at his face as I ask it so that I may see the contempt he has for my interest in his mode of transportation. I look at him, struggling to control a quivering muscle at the corner of my mouth. Is it a smile? 'Do you have a car?' I ask again.

His mouth is thick, slightly pursed, skeptical. 'No,' he says.

I look at the form I am filling out. I don't believe he doesn't have a car. I think he is only saying this because he believes that if he has a car I will tell him he isn't eligible for assistance. It makes no difference whether he has a car or not, it's one of the few things he is allowed to have. The question is on the form purely as a formality, or on the long shot that someone who has two cars will own to both of them. Two cars are not allowed. With two cars I could sign the bottom of the application and send him on his way without a pang of guilt. I could even go back to my desk and tell the man who sits next to me, 'two cars, two new cars and neither of them paid for,' and we could smile over such folly.

My pen is still lingering at the beginning of the question about the car. 'You can have a car,' I explain to him. 'It doesn't make any difference. You can have a car and still be eligible.'

He leans back in his chair appraising me. My veiled accusation hasn't escaped him. 'I don't have a car,' he says.

I move to the next question. This is the question that always causes trouble. It reads, 'Does anyone on the household have a credit card in the name of someone who is not in the household?' When I read this as it is most people think I am asking if they have a stolen credit card, an idea that infuriates them. I solve this dilemma by asking for any kind of credit card, and if the client has one (this is rare) I look at the name on it. 'Do you have a credit card?' I inquire.

He sniffs to show how foolish this question is, how clearly a waste of time. 'No,' he says, 'no credit card and no bank account.'

It is hot in the room where we are sitting. I would like to take off my sweater but I don't want this man to see me removing even the most innocent article of clothing. I don't want to inflame him. We are alone, the door is shut, and we are mercilessly close together. If I shout, of course, help will come immediately. There is a bigger black man outside the door, paid by the state to protect me in such a situation. If I should shout he would throw the door open and, without asking any questions, drag whoever was sitting with me out of the room. He would be angry, and this man would certainly be angry, so there might be a fight, at the very least a punch in the face, possibly bloodshed. That is why I must be very careful not to shout, no matter how hot it gets in here. I must not raise my voice until his hand is firmly closed around my throat. Then I must scream as loud and long as I can.

We complete the application. He is carefully filling out a form I have given him, a form which asks, among other personal questions, what grade of school he has completed. I am interested to see what he will put in this blank. I speculate that he has finished high school and so I am surprised at the big round eight he sets in the appropriate block. He looks up at me, his tongue wedged against his teeth in concentration. He doesn't like me to see the trouble this form is causing him. The questions are vague, VETERANS' STATUS, EMPLOYMENT REGISTRANT, the print is small and the blanks for the answers are too short. His patience has worn thin long ago. 'Just put the month and the year,' I say as his pen pauses over DATE OF LAST EMPLOYMENT. He writes the numbers quickly, then pushes the form towards me. We are both relieved, since the completion of this form means we are done with each other.

Except for the stairs. He is a big strong man and there is no doubt in my mind that he can find his way down the staircase and out into the street. But it is the conviction of both the black and the white heads of this department that if a client is left alone on the stairs he is likely to 'loiter' or worse still, 'wander about.' So I must escort him to the door. He doesn't seem to know this, he is pulling himself out of his chair in an obvious hurry to go. 'Wait a minute,' I say, pushing my papers into my manila folder. 'I'll go downstairs with you.'

It is my habit to walk up the stairs behind the client and down in front of him. This keeps the client from unwonted speculation about my back as it rises before him and invites him to feel superior to me as he follows me down, a sentiment which I encourage since the interview is concluded and I have gotten what I wanted. Most clients allow two or three steps between us as we make our way up and down, but this man is so close behind me I can feel his breath on my neck. The stairwell is ugly, the walls are peeling and spotted, the steps are strewn with cigarette butts and other less identifiable items. I am not nervous, but relieved. For me the stretch of staircase is already over. I am thinking I must remind the man to send me his rent receipt before he goes out the door. I am thinking that as soon as he is gone I can eat the unexciting sandwich which waits for me in my desk drawer. My foot misses a step. There is a moment when my entire body is poised impossibly in space, tensing for the grand crush of gravity that will drive me forward and down over the stairs. My arms rise up like wings that would rescue me, hold me in flight if they could, and at the peak of the arc my left arm is making in the air, I am aware of a hand closing on my elbow. The pressure is light at first, then suddenly hard, as if the hand had expected to catch something bigger than what it caught. I turn slightly on the stair and my balance is checked, thanks to the support of the hand on my elbow, which I can see now, large and black. Past that I can see the man's face from which all expression has been drained, save one, concern. This expression complicates even as I watch, as it becomes clear to us both that I will not fall and that his hand, which is still gripping my elbow, has no reason to be there. 'Take it easy,' he laughs, releasing me.

We pull ourselves together and apart. I continue down the stairs and he doesn't follow me so closely. I am flushed and hot with confusion. I have seen his face filled with tenderness and surprise over the flimsiness of my elbows, my thin white bones, and he has seen in my eyes a rush of gratitude and confidence. In fact we have defied together, among other laws, the laws of gravity, and we are shy to look at each other, ashamed of our momentary complicity. At the bottom of the stairs he passes me quickly and goes out onto the street. I turn back to the staircase, forgetting all about the rent receipt, so eager are we both to be free of the sight of one another.

SURFACE CALM

Ellen found the chain in the closet. At one time, it had hung from the ceiling in the hall, serving to pull the attic door open, a light tarnished gold chain with square jagged links. She drew it across her hand, examining the hook at one end, then passed it around her waist. It didn't quite reach. She pulled her sweater up and hooked it about her waist, pulling in her breath to make it fit. When she let her breath out it held, but cut painfully into her side. 'I should keep it on,' she thought as she unfastened it, 'to remind me to stand straight.' She dropped the chain on the end of the bed, picked up a long flannel gown and went into the bathroom.

She glanced at the mirror, remembering something she had heard as a child, something about still water, like glass. Water was sometimes like glass, she thought, clear and smooth, giving a perfect reflection. Imperfection came from beneath, causing undulations, riffling the smooth surface.

The phone rang and she ran to silence it, not saying 'hello' but 'yes' because when she had pulled the gown over her head, she thought she had heard someone call her name.

'Ellen?' Neil said. 'Ellen, are you all right?'

'Yes, yes, I'm all right.'

'You sounded so strange.'

'A little spooky I guess. Where are you?'

'Oh, in New York. I just got in. The plane was stacked up for an hour.'

'Stacked up?'

'Yes, you know. Flying around in circles because there wasn't room to land.'

'Oh yes, of course. You're all right then?'

'I guess so. If I can just find a cab to get to the hotel.'

'You're still in the airport?'

'Yes. I – well, I don't know. All the way up here I was afraid something had happened to you. I don't know why. Just a feeling.'

'What could happen to me,' she said without much humour. 'You're the one flying around in machines.'

'Nothing I guess. Silly I guess.'

'When will you be back?' she asked though she knew he didn't know. It was only that she could think of nothing else to say.

'I don't know. I'll find out at the first meeting.'

'Well, call me when you find out.'

'Yes, I will. I guess I'd better go. This is getting expensive.'

'All right. Good night dear.'

'Yes, I'll call tomorrow night.'

'All right.'

'Good. Don't worry about me.'

'I won't.'

'All right then, good night.' He hung up.

As she returned the receiver to the cradle she reflected that she could think of no reason to worry about him. She sat down on the bed, leaned forward to turn off the light and noticed the chain, curled on the foot of the bed where she had left it. 'I don't know,' she said after a moment. She was cold. She picked up the chain, hooked it about her waist beneath her gown and reached for the light switch a second time. The chain dug into her side and she winced. When she lay on her back in the darkness her hands sought out the offending links and adjusted them as comfortably as was possible. She thought only momentarily of Neil, of the time difference in New York and then she drifted into a stark and dreamless sleep.

She had only a vague idea in mind when she put on the chain and in the morning she could not remember why she had done it. She took a shower, laying the chain on top of her folded gown, determining that she would not put it on again. She washed the red track round her waist carefully, noting without much surprise, that in several places the links had broken the skin. She tried again but could think of no reasonable explanation for having done it. Finally, after three cups of coffee and a slice of toast she wandered into the bathroom and put the chain on again, just as she had before. As it didn't seem very tight she moved the hook on a link. The pain was reassuring. She dismissed her concern and went outside to work in the garden.

She didn't leave the area of the house all that day and as the afternoon progressed she began to relax in the quiet around her. She spoke out loud twice. First, when she was standing on her toes, reaching for the rose clippers in the garden shed. She could only reach the shelf with her hands and was forced to feel about among the spades and old packs of seeds until she lost her balance and sat down hard on the lawnmower. 'Well,' she said out of breath, 'you can't do it.'

Later, considering what she would have for dinner (poised before the shelves and shelves of boxes and cans in the pantry), she realized with pleasant bitterness that she would be eating alone. 'It doesn't matter,' she said without noticing that she was speaking. 'Anything will do.' She decided on a salad as it was the easiest to prepare. Nor would she eat at six but at seven, as she had done before she was married.

She was slicing a tomato when the phone rang.

'Ellen?' he said. He never said hello. He thought it inefficient.

'Yes dear,' she said. 'How are you?'

'All right, I guess. I've been in a meeting for six hours.'

'You must be exhausted,' She picked up the knife and cleaned the tomato off the blade with a paper towel.

'It looks like we'll be finished here next Thursday,' he said.

'Is that definite?' She shifted her weight from one foot to the other and leaned against the wall between the refrigerator and the counter.

'I think so. Are you all right?'

'Yes, of course.'

'What did you do today?'

'Nothing much. I fooled around in the garden. I was just fixing something to eat.'

'This late?'

'What time is it?'

'Nearly eight, your time.'

'Well, I was reading. I must have lost track.'

'I miss you,' he blurted softly, conspiratorially. 'And I've only been gone one day.'

She began to feel as is she were standing inside the refrigerator instead of against it. She closed her eyes and pressed the blade of the knife against her forefinger. When she opened her eyes the blade was smeared with red. 'I miss you too,' she said without effort. She smiled, then frowned, adding more seriously, with emphasis, 'I really do.'

'Well, it isn't so long,' he reassured her. 'I guess it's just that we've never been apart before.'

She saw herself then, running to meet him at the door of her mother's house, years ago, a childish woman with narrow features and wide eyes. 'Neil,' she said. She was close to tears. 'I've never been alone before.'

'Are you sure you're all right? Maybe you should come up here.'

She knew he didn't mean it. They had settled it all before. It was too expensive. 'No,' she said, 'no, I'm just being silly. I'm all right, I'm fine. But call tomorrow, won't you?'

'Sure,' he said. 'Sure I will. I'll call every night. And I'll be home before you know.'

When she hung up she felt as if her face had frozen. She pressed her cheek against the refrigerator and examined the still-bleeding cut on her finger. Then she picked up the knife and made a quick slice on the next finger, holding the blade sideways, like a razor and slitting the skin sharply so that it left a stinging cut. She did the next finger and the next. When she had finished both her hands her forehead was cool and damp and she went into the bathroom to bandage the cuts.

That evening she ate her dinner quietly, stripped as mindlessly as a nun and went to bed in her chain and bandaged fingers. In the morning she woke to find her hands throbbing. After her shower she moved the chain up a few inches and took the bandages off her fingers. The cuts were open but bloodless. She spent the morning washing clothes, a job which consisted, for the most part, of leaning listlessly against the churning machine. After another salad for lunch she sat down to sew buttons on a long neglected pile of clothing but her hands hurt so badly that she gave up on the second shirt. She sat for awhile, staring into space, absently jabbing the needle into the back of her hand. When she looked down she found a little line of red dots running from knuckle to knuckle and down to the base of her wrist. The sight of them made her uncomfortable and she hurried to the kitchen to wash off the blood. Then she grabbed her purse and ran out of the house, not really knowing where she was going or why.

She felt better as soon as she was in the car and made the stops and turns that led to the grocery store, as if she were a horse whose life was one routine. Inside the vegetables were gleaming but the people around her were harried, impatient, disgruntled. The checkout girl scowled at her lettuce and tomatoes as if they had misbehaved, then looked at her as if she were a negligent mother. She went outside and stood under the store awning for nearly a minute before she realized it was raining. She spotted the hardware store and, pulling her collar up and her chin down, began to thread her way through the parking lot, hesitantly, as if it were a crowd of people.

The hardware store was dark and musty as a cellar, smelling of fertilizer, mold and decay. If the man who moved towards her from the black depths of shovels and bags had looked any more like a toad she would have laughed. As it was, the greenish pallor of his skin filled her with an uneasy nausea. When he spoke his voice was a patronizing croak and she backed away, thinking that he had jumped at her. 'Yes,' she answered his bulging-eyed inquiry, 'I want some rope and a length of wire and, let's see, some thumb tacks.'

'What kind of rope?'

She found herself smiling deep into his liquid bulbous eyes. 'How many kinds of rope are there?'

'All kinds: packing rope, sailing cord, different weights, different textures.'

'I'll have to have a look at it,' she said, following him to the back of the place where he showed her a display of ropes that amazed her. She picked out a rough, fairly thick packing rope, the kind that comes on brown paper packages and ravels on the edges.

When he showed her his collection of wire she began to feel giddy. Fascinated by the various barbed wires she ran her hands over the little prongs. The toad-man inclined his head towards her with the slow intoxicated smile of a pimp who lives in a dream of the seduction he sells.

When she got home she dropped the vegetables into the refrigerator drawer and, clutching her bag of supplies, hurried to the bathroom. Her reflection loomed towards her in the half-light and she stopped to look at herself. Her face was holding up fairly well.

There had been a time when mirrors offered her more satisfaction than now. In a few years, she thought, she would be like all those other middle-aged women who look at their reflections only under extreme provocation, at which time they ignore the eyes and examine the makeup instead of the face. She opened her eyes wide then dropped them halfway and gave herself the delicately breathless smile she reserved for moments of the keenest pleasure. She looked away impatiently, took off her blouse and began unraveling the wire.

Days and days passed and still she did not stop, nor did she conclude that something was inexplicably wrong. It was only that the explanation would take time and that her time was rapidly becoming the province and property of sleep. She slept twelve hours a night and two or three more in the afternoon. In her waking hours her head hurt constantly and she barely had the energy to move from place to place. This pain lessened as the days passed and the marks of her ritual, which multiplied daily, became her only source of consolation for the hours in which her eyes were open. Neil called every day and each time had less to say. He was perpetually cheerful and she was monosyllabic. When he announced that he would be home the following day she woke up for the first time in a week. 'What time does you plane get in?' she asked and her voice was so flat that it frightened her.

'Nine o'clock. Will you come to meet me?'

'Yes, yes of course. I'll be there.'

'Good,' he said. 'I can barely wait to see you. I'm so glad this thing is almost over.'

When he hung up, she retained the receiver for a moment, thinking that the buzzing was coming from the inside of her head. In a sudden panic she ran to the bathroom and took off the chain, unhooked the wire and took the band-aids off the backs of her knees and ankles, exposing the four meticulous slices she had made while shaving the night before. Then she took off all her clothes and looked at herself in the full length mirror on the door. 'It's almost over,' she said. She noticed that through some oversight or secret timidity she had spared her breasts. She examined the cuts around her waist and strained her neck to see the jagged red lines on her shoulders. There was no way on earth to make them heal by the next evening. As long as she had her clothes on she was safe. But how long would that last? He'd been away, he'd been faithful, she was sure of that. He would require some assurance that there was sufficient reason for his fidelity and, of course, if she turned him down he would be more surprised than he was sure to be by the sight of her maligned body, for she had never turned him down before. Her only hope lay in darkness and that was not likely. For reasons she had never been able to comprehend Neil preferred to 'see what he was doing,' and their lovemaking always transpired beneath the glare of an overhead light. 'When he sees this,' she said, referring to her body as if it were the remains of his favorite chair. 'Oh Christ, when he sees this.'

The airport was crowded. Neil came at her from a whirl of hair and eyes, his arms outstretched, his teeth exposed in a welcoming grin that turned into a most unwelcome embrace.

Beneath the tightening of his arms she felt her wounds re-open, popping like flowers, one by one. He slid his arm across her shoulder and ushered her through the crowd. By the time they reached the car she was convinced that she was soaked in blood, but found, when she had a chance to look, that it was sweat. Neil didn't notice. He said he was ecstatic and what did she think of his mustache. It was a surprise for her and when the full impact of his efforts to grow it and his desire to please her finally hit, she burst into laughter.

'You don't like it?' he said, pushing the hopeless little growth into a semblance of order with the assistance of the car mirror. 'You really don't like it. I'll shave it right off as soon as we get home.'

'No,' she said. 'I love it. It looks wonderful. It's just that – it's just that –'

'Just that what?' he inquired with a petulant look.

'That it's such a surprise.' Her voice went all wrong. It was hollow, insincere. She clapped a hand over her offending mouth.

But he hadn't noticed. He was busy backing out of the parking lot. Once on the road he gave her a self-conscious smile. 'I thought you'd be surprised,' he said.

When they got home he threw his suitcase across the bed and turned to her as if he intended to throw her after it. She backed up until she hit the wall. He sat down and began taking off his shoes and socks while she stood watching, looking all round his face, at his hair, his nose, his mustache, carefully avoiding the eyes which were searching her own. She was ready to scream. When he crossed the room and kissed her she kept her lips fastened together. He held her at arm's length and gave her such a look that she threw her arms around his neck and kissed him as passionately as she could, trying with all her strength to swallow him whole so that she would not have to look at him looking at her. Again he held her at arm's length and made a question of his eyes, but soft this time, the kind of question that invites only one response, like asking a child it he wants ice cream. She looked down. He unbuttoned her blouse and pushed it aside without looking, finding the first two cuts with his fingers. She continued looking down. The he backed away, pushing the blouse back with his hands and looking beneath it with all his eyes. 'Jesus Christ,' he said and she felt his hands go slack around her waist. He turned away and stood with his back to her. Still she did not look up.

'Who did that?' he said in a tone she did not recognize, one capable of outrage. He turned around and his face was white. 'Who did that to you?' he said again.

'No one,' she said.

'No one?' he shouted. 'Look at you!' He ripped off the blouse and began working at the skirt. When he saw her waist he made a choking sound and his cheeks flushed with a dull grey color. 'God, Ellen. Look at you.'

'I did it myself,' she said and, as if to spite her, her mouth smiled.

'*You* did this?' he said. 'You did this to yourself? But why? Why would you do something like this?'

'I don't know,' she replied. 'I don't know why I did it. If I knew why I wouldn't have had to do it.'

'What? What does that mean?'

She wondered why she was not crying. 'Oh Neil.' She said. 'I've been so frightened.' She tried to catch his eyes with her own but his gaze was riveted to her waist. She turned to the wall, realizing too late that her back was as unpleasant as the front of her, that it would only shock him. She heard him gasp and she hid her face in her hands. Then for the first time in weeks her body did the right thing, it shuddered and it started to cry. She turned around to show him the tears and he motioned her into his arms. She cried for a long time and he held her quietly, saying things she did not hear, stroking her hair, indulging her with the combination of fear and satisfaction that men have for women whom they have driven to hysterics.

When she was calm again, they talked quietly for awhile and he decided that she would have to go to two doctors the very next day, one for her head and one for 'what you've done to yourself.' She said that she thought she would be all right now that he was back, that it was just the loneliness that had made her act so rashly, that she had tried to tell him on the phone but couldn't bring herself to. He nodded and agreed, but when she looked at him she saw that he thought she was completely insane. What bothered her more was that she understood in the same glance that though he was convinced that she was mad he still wished to make love to her. She shrugged and looked away, apologized, explained herself again and in the end avoided his eyes and reclined beneath the weight of his insistence.

In the morning she got up first and dressed in the patterned darkness of early morning light filtered through slatted blinds. He got up when he heard her fixing breakfast and stumbled into the kitchen only half-awake. He asked her to take his shirts to the cleaners. Afterwards she sat at the table and listened to him singing in the shower, thinking that he had forgotten the whole thing, that it was not as if she was real at all. But when he kissed her good-bye at the door he surprised her, for he touched her as if he thought she might break. He took her face in his hands and spoke to her with an intensity she did not know how to receive. 'I'll come home for lunch,' he said. 'If you feel strange, or afraid, or like you might do something desperate, call me, all right?'

'Yes,' she said. 'I will.'

'Promise me, now.'

'Yes, I promise.'

'Good. Do you feel all right?'

'Yes, I feel fine.'

'Maybe we can get through this thing without doctors. Do you think so?'

'Yes.'

He turned to go.

'Neil,' she said. 'I'm sorry. I'm so sorry.'

'It's all right,' he said. 'I never should have left you like that.'

'But how could you have known?'

'That's what I'm trying to figure out,' he said in perfect seriousness. 'I think I should have. But I just didn't.'

After he was gone she busied herself with cleaning the house. She decided to paint the bedroom another color, a real color this time, instead of the off-white-nearly-a-color of all the rooms in the house. She decided upon yellow, a real vibrant yellow, almost gold, like the sun. The trouble with their house was that it was always cold, no matter what the temperature. When she had finished cleaning she went outside and sat in the sun, where Neil found her when he came home. She'd forgotten about lunch. They went to a restaurant and she felt wonderful, wide awake and so hungry that she wanted to eat everything on every plate that she saw on the other tables. Neil was inordinately gay, telling her amusing stories about the horrors of New York nightclubs and the aging business men he had been forced to entertain. He left her at the house afterwards and asked again if she was all right. She assured him that she was, sincerely, happily and with a feeling of elation that swept her close to tears. She spent the afternoon looking through a cookbook for something different to fix for dinner. She wanted something heavy, something with a sauce, a dish that would stand on its own, without salad, the thought of which revolted her. She began to think that she was someone else, someone she had read about. The cuts were healing and she saw herself as one just coming to life, slowly but with great promise, from the inside out.

In a week the ordeal seemed a thing of the distant past. She was possessed of a sudden affection for Neil that amazed and pleased him. And when he was gone she took to going over things he had said, things he had done, convincing herself again and again, by recalling a nod, a smile, a half-conscious caress, that he loved her to the exclusion of all else and that he thought her the perfect wife. He came home for lunch every day and called her for a few minutes in the afternoon. They did not talk about her miraculous recovery, partly because she did not want to be reminded of it and partly because neither of them really believed that she had ever been ill.

Two weeks later he called her from work to tell her that though he wanted to, he could not possibly leave and would have to miss lunch. She assured him that she did not mind and, after hanging up, assured herself of the same thing until she believed it. It was just as well as she was not hungry. She felt chilled and went outside to see the garden. The sun outside was not warm enough to please her. The rose bushes were running wild along the fence sticking out in all directions and although she found that she didn't really feel like doing much of anything she decided they would have to be cut. When she went into the shed to get the shears she was enveloped in a sudden rush of cold and dusty air, followed by a more unnerving and chilling memory that gripped her about the waist and wrists as if to pull her down.

She found the shears and hurried back to the roses, shivering and uncomfortable. She began cutting haphazardly, pushing the shears in and out of the bushes, catching the broken limbs as they fell. The sun was not warm enough to please her. She was aware that the thorns were cutting her hands, that she was crushing the branches against her bare arm, that the bushes were taking on a shape that had nothing to do with the desired form. She threw the shears on the ground and sat down, gathering the branches into her lap and stripping the thorns off with her fingers, pressing them between her palms until her hands stung and burned and bled warmly and she found herself laughing and crying in alternate bursts of fear and pleasure, anger and relief.

MESSENGERS

Jacob saw the messengers when he opened the kitchen door. There were three of them, standing together in the far corner of the room, in the midst of conversation.

When the tallest of the three noticed Jacob, who stood shocked still in the doorway, he turned to the other two and said, 'It's awake.'

Jacob feigned outrage. 'What is this?' he demanded. His knees were weak and he could hear his heart thumping feebly in his ears. He dug his nails into the palms of his hands to be certain that he was awake.

The three creatures stepped away from the corner in unison, focusing their attention upon him. The tallest, who was the spokesman for the group, stretched his hand out, palm upward. Jacob backed away from the proffered hand, partly in fear, and partly in fascination. The creatures' fingers were webbed together with a film-like substance that glistened as if it were wet. All along his arm the film hung in loose folds. When he raised his arm, these folds pulled into a diaphanous, almost liquid sheet that extended from his waist to the diamond bright material of his torso. Jacob attempted to communicate his surprise by looking into the creature's face, only to find his terror doubly reflected in the pupils of two shining silver eyes. He closed his own eyes and covered them with his hands.

'Jacob Abel?' a human voice inquired. Jacob uncovered his eyes but kept them fastened upon the long transparent toes of his interlocutor.

'You are Jacob Abel?' the voice inquired again. Jacob nodded.

'He's afraid,' one of the others observed. At this remark the three burst into childish titters. Jacob took courage and looked up. 'Sorry to come at you like this,' the spokesman apologized, stepping back a bit. 'Suppose we stand still and close our eyes and you can have a good look at us.'

Jacob looked, but he could make no sense of what he saw. They were all much taller than he, the tallest being nearly seven feet, but they didn't look particularly powerful. In fact they were pitifully emaciated, the hollows in their cheeks and below their eyes being unusually deep and of a sickly rose color. The tallest opened one silver eye and surveyed Jacob's reaction. 'Can you speak?' he asked.

Jacob cleared his throat. 'Yes.'

'Good.' They all relaxed, opening their wide eyes and blinking rapidly.

'We know we look odd,' the spokesman continued. 'But it's only through the grace of God that we are able to materialize at all.'

'I'm hallucinating,' Jacob said drily.

'You're not hallucinating,' the other corrected him.

'Oh yes I am,' Jacob insisted. He passed in front of them and went to the stove. 'I'd better drink some coffee.'

The three held a brief conference. 'What can we do to convince you that we're real?' the tallest asked from the midst of his counsel.

Jacob put the kettle on the burner and took the coffee filter out of the drawer nearest him. 'There's nothing you can do,' he answered.

'Absolutely nothing. So why don't you just go away?'

'Perhaps if you touched us—'

Jacob faced the creatures angrily. 'If I could hallucinate something that looked like you, I could certainly hallucinate something that felt – however it is you feel.' He turned away again, overcome by a rush of exquisitely confusing scents. 'Or smell,' he added.

The creatures conferred again. 'Will you do what we tell you to do?' the spokesman asked.

Jacob poured the coffee into a cup and sucked at the scalding liquid. He turned to scowl at the question without speaking.

'Have you no fear for your soul?'

Jacob sniffed.

'You're about to go out into the worst day of your life.'

'I can see that,' Jacob said flatly. He reasoned that an hallucination couldn't really do him any physical damage. The best thing was to try to ignore it. With this in mind he turned away just as the tallest creature was about to speak, and carefully measured a teaspoon full of sugar into his cup. When he had done this he stirred the coffee slowly, counting aloud the number of little circles he was making. When he looked back he was relieved to find himself the object of the confused gaze of his wife, who leaned in the doorway of the otherwise empty room.

'Who are you talking to?' she asked sleepily.

'No one,' he said, adding as an afterthought, 'Myself.'

An hour later Jacob arrived at his office. He told his secretary to hold all calls and sat at his desk quietly for about twenty minutes. In that time he went over everything that had transpired in the kitchen that morning. He congratulated himself for having kept his suspicion from his wife until he had thought it out thoroughly. From all the evidence he could come up with, he had been the victim of a real multisensual hallucination. 'A real hallucination,' he said out loud. He realized that he had feared, even expected, such an occurrence for as long as he had known the phenomena was possible. 'The fear of it must have caused it,' he told himself. He would have to go to a psychiatrist; he would probably have to go into debt, tell his wife, maybe even lose his job. The prospect had some vague attraction for him. He was looking at the list of psychiatrists' names in the yellow pages when the intercom rang.

He switched it on and said tersely, 'No calls, Nancy.'

Nancy spoke with hushed excitement. 'It's an emergency call for you,' she said. 'From Mercy Hospital.'

Jacob switched to the call and listened blankly as a doctor informed him that his wife was being admitted to the hospital. There had been an accident, the calm voice informed him, she had been thrown from the car.

'Is she all right?' he asked, then rephrased the question to suit the ominous silence on the other end of the line. 'Is she badly hurt?'

The voice paused. 'Yes,' it continued. Jacob felt a choking sensation in his throat. 'How fast can you get here?'

He didn't reply but threw the receiver on the desk and ran away from it, through the office, past his startled secretary and out into the street.

Inside the cab he pleaded with the driver to go as fast as he could, shoving the money into the man's astonished hands, twenty dollars. In the ten minutes it took to get from his office to the hospital he experienced enough anguish to know how inextricably he was bound to his wife. He ran up the stairs and into the reception room. By the time the nurse had told him what floor to go to, he was conscious of nothing but her name, Christina, which he repeated over and over like a litany.

When the elevator doors opened he was nearly deafened by the screams. A doctor led him down the hall, past two doors which served to lower the volume of the cries as they were closed behind him. Jacob didn't know exactly when he had started sweating, but as he allowed himself to be seated in a leather chair, he was aware that his face was streaming. Though he knew he had never heard anything as frightening as the sounds that came at him through the closed doors, he recognized them as a perversion of Christina's voice. He tried to listen to what the doctor was telling him.

The accident, the doctor explained, was a head-on collision. Christina had been slammed through the front window of the car. Somehow her arm had been caught around the steering wheel. When the wheel didn't give, Christina's arm did. It was almost completely torn off at the elbow. She had suffered as well, a fractured jaw, a broken back, and several deep lacerations. The problem they faced now, the doctor told Jacob solemnly, was that, though she had suffered a great shock and though they had given her enough sedative to kill a normal person, she was still conscious. 'And,' he added, 'she is in great pain.' A silence fell between them during which Jacob listened to his wife's agonized cries. He stood up and grabbed the doctor by the shoulders, shaking him as hard as he could. 'For God's sake,' he screamed. 'Can't you knock her out, can't you help her!' The doctor struggled with him and finally freed himself. Jacob fell back into his chair, overcome by trembling.

'Do you know of any explanation for this, Mr Abel?' the doctor pleaded. 'Does anything in your wife's history –'

Jacob shook his head hopelessly.

'We don't know what to do –' He opened the door, looked out into the hall and back at Jacob. 'We don't know what to do,' he concluded weakly.

'Let me see her,' Jacob said.

He didn't recognize her, nor did she know that he was in the room. Unable to stand before the sight of her suffering he allowed himself to be led outside her door. At ten o'clock he began his vigil.

By one, her screams had scarcely weakened. Every few minutes she shaped the expression of her pain into the syllables of Jacob's name. After two or three tries, he gave up trying to tell her he was near. By five o'clock her voice was gone. Her cries were the sound of bleeding tissues being continually torn by the air forced back and forth in her throat. At six Jacob went back into the room and stood at the foot of her bed. Her struggles were confined by the straps which held her down against the sheets. She looked at him from the depths of her ravagement and tried to speak. He went to her, bent over her and made out the words, 'do what they tell you,' each word splintering the air that stood between her lips and his ear.

For two more hours he sat on a straight back chair outside her door. His jaw ached from the constant and involuntary clenching of his teeth. Twice the doctor sat down beside him, without speaking, to smoke a hurried cigarette. Jacob took up a magazine and carefully shredded the pages. The nurses passed back and forth in front of him nodding at the pile of torn colored paper accumulating between his feet, as if they found it perfectly proper. When he had finished the magazine he gathered the scraps and carried them to a trash can just past the door to Christina's room.

Then he saw them. They stood together at the end of the hall, beckoning to him with long transparent fingers. Jacob crossed the small distance between them without once thinking that he was having a hallucination. Nor did he heed an inner prompting that warned him against hope. 'Tell me what to do,' he said to the tallest of the three.

'Go to your house,' he replied. 'And burn it. Burn everything.'

Jacob nodded.

'And do it quickly.'

He took a cab to a hardware store a block from his house. There he purchased three gallons of kerosene and, encumbered with the heavy cans, he ran the rest of the way as best he could. Inside he hurried from room to room, trickling the kerosene over everything. He emptied one can on the second floor and two on the first. In the living room he stopped to snatch a photograph of Christina, but by the time he had reached the kitchen he thought better of it and threw the picture down. Then he went back upstairs with the matches. He tried a trick he hadn't done since he was in high school, standing the match against the side of the box with his index finger and flicking it into the air with his other thumb and forefinger. The tiny flame furled into the air. When it hit the kerosene soaked carpet a little line of fire sprang up, running in the direction of the bed. Jacob went methodically from room to room, flicking out matches in this fashion. As the flames filled the house with the whimpering sound of burning he was aware of a curious lightheartedness flooding through him.

He stood for a moment at the kitchen door, watching the path of the flames rush towards the table, around the legs of the chair. He ran to the end of the yard and looked back at his work.

There were flames in every window, flames already inching their way along the edge of the roof. He was so transfixed by this sight that he didn't see the woman who came running towards him from the house across the street. When she touched his elbow he turned on her quickly, seizing her outstretched hands.

'Mr Abel,' she cried out. 'Your house is burning.'

'Yes,' he shouted into her face. 'It's burning up. Can I use your phone?' She followed him to her house, shouting after him, 'the fire department number is on the pad, right next to the phone.'

Jacob called the hospital. 'Let me speak to Doctor Reed,' he said to the nurse who answered. 'This is Jacob Abel.'

There was a brief silence, in which time Jacob was dimly aware of a wave of fear, followed by another of physical nausea. 'Mr Abel,' a male voice inquired at the other end of the line.

'How is she?'

'She's unconscious, Mr Abel. She has been now for about ten minutes.'

Jacob hung up the phone and sat down on the floor. 'It worked,' he whispered. The woman stood dumbfounded in the doorway before him. He raised his arms over his head and gripped the back of his neck with both hands, hiding his face between his elbows. He rocked himself then, back and forth, weeping uncontrollably. The woman bent over him. 'Mr Abel,' she said softly. 'What is it? What's happened?'

By the time the fireman got there the house was burnt to a crisp black shell. Jacob watched them without much interest. One of the men came over to him and said sharply. 'You burned this place up, buddy. You're in a lot of trouble.'

Jacob laughed at the man. 'It was mine to burn,' he said.

Then he asked the woman who stood solicitously at his side to drive him to the hospital.

Christina's suffering had left her drawn and spectrally white. Jacob sat in the room with her unconscious body for four hours while the doctors busied themselves over her, determined to bring her back to life. Jacob watched them numbly, listening to the diminishing odds they gave him, from time to time, for her survival.

At midnight Doctor Reed took him to a doctor's lounge where they drank coffee together. Jacob washed his hands and looked at his face in the mirror over the sink. He was surprised to see his face again, surprised most of all to see that it hadn't changed. 'There's no hope now,' the doctor informed him. Jacob rubbed his knuckles into his eyes, watching the flashes of red and green that washed up behind his eyelids. In the momentary blackness that came behind these colors, Christina's presence flooded through him like a flash of light, leaving a sweet taste in his mouth, a warm lassitude in his limbs and an unfathomable serenity in his chest. To avoid looking again at his own face, lest he lose this vision, he examined his fingernails, noting the jagged lines of dirt beneath each one, pulled tentatively at the lapels of his wrinkled jacket, and turned away from his reflection to follow the white back of the doctor to Christina's door.

THE MECHANICS OF IT

This happened five years ago. I was lying in bed with Jerome and I bit him on the thigh. Before I did it I had been looking at his thigh, which was just next to my face, raised slightly above me, as his knee was bent, and it occurred to me that I would like to feel his thigh between my teeth. I leaned forward, as if to caress him, pulling his leg down over my face and then I bit him, hard, harder that I had imagined I would. What was I expecting? I expected him to shout with pain. Instead he wound his hand through my hair and pulled my head up, abruptly. I didn't resist, my head being pulled away from his leg, pulled up to where he could reach my face with his other hand, to where I could see him, smiling sleepily at me, and he slapped me across the face, hard, then let me drop. I recoiled to my place between his legs, lay curled up there, my hand covering my face, touching the place where the skin was stinging. Jerome continued to work his hand through my hair, rubbing my skull, lazily.

This was five years ago. Since then I have

married, had a child, moved away from the city where Jerome lives, changed everything. And in that time not one day (not one) has passed when I haven't dragged out this memory and examined it, gone over it, tried to bring it back to some kind of life. And not once a day. Once a day would be nothing. I could go on forever if it were only once a day. Twenty times a day, forty, God knows how many. There are days, after I have dreamed about Jerome, when I think of nothing else. Just this little scene. My teeth sinking into Jerome's thigh and the slap, delivered without particular passion, lazily, the way a lioness slaps down her misbehaving cub. On these days anything that distracts me from this memory is an annoyance. I can barely tolerate having to eat on these days.

I am thinking about this now, as I help my daughter pull on her rubber boots so that she can go out and play in the snow. I am going over it, my teeth in Jerome's thigh, his smile, the slap. She is in a hurry. This is the first snow of the year. There are other children in the front yard already, pelting one another with little fistfuls of snow, too fine to pack; it falls apart in the air. She and I watched the children from the front window, and I agreed that she could go out. 'Hurry, Mommy,' she says now. 'Hurry up.'

As I have reached the part when my face is being pulled away from Jerome's thigh and I am smiling back at him and his hand is just leaving the sheet on its way to the side of my face, I shake her a little by the shoulders, teasing her. 'Are you in such a hurry to get away from me?' I ask, teasing her.

She doesn't care for my teasing. Outside the other children are shouting and that is all she hears. 'My gloves,' she says, seriously, 'Where are my gloves?'

Her gloves are on the piano. I give her the left and then the right one and she pulls them on, anxious. If I were to tell her she could not go out to the other children she would become so angry at me she wouldn't be able to control herself. I have seen her like this, in a rage at me, biting her own knuckles and pulling at her hair because she is afraid to do what she would like to do, kick at me and leave, laugh at me. She is like me. I tie her hat under her chin and kiss her, hold her to me. 'What are you thinking?' I ask her. She squirms in my arms. 'Mommy, please,' she complains. I let her go.

I stand in the window and watch her painful progress through the snow. She falls, gets up, falls again. Her friends are not particularly interested in her arrival, though they see her, they know she is coming, and they don't mind. I like to watch her when she is running to me, when I catch her up and hold her so that her heart beats against me, just under my own heart, but it hurts me to see her running away, so confidently, to her indifferent companions.

At the edge of the yard I see the mailman, trudging through the snow towards our house, a bundle of letters in his lands. Letters for us. The children run across his path, fall in his path, wave at him. Will there be a letter from Jerome?

When I am restless, as I am now, (though I don't know why I should be restless) I run my hands through my hair and rub my skull with my fingertips the way Jerome did, after he slapped me. It comforts me to do this. I remember how I felt, when he did this, after I bit him so hard, after he slapped me, as I lay curled between his legs and he rubbed my skull, winding his big hand through my hair. I felt that I had been moving towards this feeling since I was a child, like my daughter, running out to her friends, I was going to Jerome, for two minutes (was it two minutes?) of satiation.

Oh yes, I am sighing, as the mailman opens the box and drops a few envelopes inside. I wave to him, he nods at me. He imagines that I am lazy, standing in the window in my robe at 11:00 in the morning. Is he wishing I would ask him to come in? Give him some coffee? Talk about the mail? Is he wondering if my husband is home?

My husband is at the table, working over his papers. He shuffles through the papers, mumbles to himself, then begins again. I watch him at his work, watch him until he looks up at me, smiles at me. I am standing at the window, rubbing my hands against my skull, sighing to myself, and this interests him. He likes to see me when I am restless like this, though it frightens him. I smile, opening my robe at the top, suggestively. This shocks him, for I am standing at the window. Suppose someone should see me?

I go to him, stand behind his chair, wrap my arms around his shoulders, and press my lips against his neck, his cheek, forehead, my teeth bared and clenched. This worries him. He is happy with me and with his daughter. He likes nothing better than to see us together, walking together, walking towards him. Or laughing together. Now he is a little frightened for he can feel my restlessness, though my kisses, through the roughness of my hands moving down his chest. Who will protect him from me? His daughter is outside with her friends, the mailman has come and gone, leaving the letter from Jerome that will make all this impossible, this bitter embracing. I cover the beginnings of his protest with my tongue, and he gives in, closes his eye, forgets about his fear. So we are deep in this kiss, I am deep in it. I can feel Jerome's hand, just behind my head, moving towards my hair. In a moment I will be pulled away from this, better hang on to it, and slapped, harder than I can prepare for.

Later I will go through the letters twice, reading the return addresses, before I hand the stack to my husband. 'Anything interesting?' he will ask, looking at the letters, looking at me. And I will shrug. 'You are restless today,' he will observe, amused, a little annoyed. 'What makes you so restless?'

And I will laugh. 'I don't know,' I will say.

I can't think of any explanation for this.

CONTRACTION

Marta looked up from her book. The man sitting next to her leaned away, correcting the balance between them. He had been trying to read the title on the top of the page. Marta closed the book and slipped it into her bag, careful not to let him see the title. 'He's wondering what it was,' she thought. 'What was she reading?' He had seen her biting her lip over the paragraph she had just finished.

Biting her lip and closing her eyes for a moment, and then beginning the paragraph over again. The paragraph had shocked her. She felt as if every third or fourth paragraph in that book was a new, different, unpleasant and inexplicable shock. The book was written by a woman. 'Just another woman wrote the book,' she thought. So how could this be a shock? What was it about another woman who wrote books, what was it about what she wrote that shocked Marta, who sat on the streetcar on the way to see her lover and who was not easily shocked? Who was sympathetic with everyone but herself? This woman's book shocked her right to her bones and she could feel her back going stiff and her teeth grinding harder and harder, tasting and testing, working her lower lip over the book so that people tried to get in position to see the title. They saw that she was shocked by what she read; they wanted to know what it was.

She didn't want anyone to know about the book and how badly it was shocking her. 'Why not?' she thought. 'It's not an obscene book. It's just a book of stories written by a woman who is probably, who must be, very like me.' What shocked Marta most was the thought of how much she must be like the author. She wanted to write a letter to the woman. 'Who are you and why are you writing these stories that are so shocking, so inexcusable? Why can't you keep this sort of thing to yourself?' The woman must not have any life at all, Marta thought. The book proved that. Everything that happened to the author, everything she saw, was material for the book. She couldn't have a life. She talked about lovers, she talked about fear, she talked about children and pain and violence, a lot of violence, curtly presented, neatly dispensed with, the kind of violence that woke Marta from sour, poisonous dreams at night and sent her spilling out of sleep, soured, unnatural and shocked, as she was by the book, shocked by the content of her dreams.

'It's too close to home.' It occurred to her that she should throw the book away, because it was hurting her to read about herself, about her dreams, every day. Every day, she read another story in the book and it was always the same. She took out the book and looked at the table of contents. There were twenty stories, she had read eleven. For eleven days she had been reading the book and now she saw that she would have nine more days, a story a day, and then she would be done with the book. 'And done with that woman,' she thought, 'for good.'

Perhaps she would write a letter to the woman. But she was not the kind of person who wrote letters to writers, or to anyone else whom she didn't really know. Though when she got through the next nine days, 'a story a day,' she thought, she would know the woman who wrote the book as well as she had known anyone in her life.

But it was a mistake to think that. The book was fiction. The woman had probably never even had some of the experiences she described in the book. She may never have had a lover. Marta remembered that she had read somewhere, or someone had told her, that the woman had no children. And another friend, who had gone to school with someone who had been in a class with the woman who wrote the book, had told her that the woman was like a computer. When she wanted to write a research paper she just put the information into her brain, which ran like a computer, and in a few days out came the research paper, and it was always good. In fact, it was a scandal how well and how much and how consistently the woman turned out columns and research articles and stories and novels. The woman wrote too much. It wouldn't be possible for her to have a life. She got up every morning and drank three cups of coffee, ate a piece of toast and wandered into her typewriter, looked at a calendar, read over what she had finished writing the night before, just as the sun came up (for the woman must sleep very little) and then she began to write. And she wrote all day, except for an hour in which she did research and another hour in which she greeted her husband and shared a hurried dinner.

But the woman was also a professor, Marta thought. She had to be at the university a few hours a day. She taught writing, she had to read the writing of her students, and she had to talk with them about their work.

Really the woman was too much. Marta wished that she could call her up and have lunch with her and talk about how she was managing to do so much and find out, perhaps she could find out, why she was so willing to give up her life for a bunch of fiction, for a bunch of stories. No time for lovers, no time for children, no time for anything but keeping her eyes and ears open and looking out for material and fictionalizing everything.

But perhaps the woman told the truth. Certainly she changed people's names and their hair colors. Marta thought it most amusing that most of the women in the book had blonde or red hair. The picture on the back of the book showed the author, wide-eyed, distinctly intelligent, watchful, even wary, looking out from underneath brown bangs. So she disguised herself, called herself a blonde, but it was really herself in all the stories. Even when the character was a man he always had wide eyes, like the author, slightly protruding eyes, with blonde or red hair. Perhaps the woman who wrote the book had a secretary and she dictated the tales of her affairs, of her fears, of her slightly rotten dreams, to her secretary, between appointments with lovers and friends everywhere.

Marta stood up and made her way to the back of the streetcar. The people looked at her as she made her way along the aisle. She brushed against a man's suit sleeve, brown tweed, too heavy for the hot day; she saw the sleeve in the corner of her eye and next to the sleeve the leg of the pants and next to the leg the bulging stomach of the woman who sat next to the man. A pregnant woman, Marta saw, and the sight made her wince. 'That woman is pregnant,' she was thinking as the doors flew open in front of her and the step dropped down and the car lurched to a stop.

She turned the key in the lock of the door to her lover's apartment. She had an idea. She could read two stories a day and then three on the last day and in this way she would be finished with the book in four, instead of nine days. It would be easy to do. The stories weren't too long.

Inside Gene lay face down on a mattress. He turned over and yawned at her. 'Are you still in bed?' she said. She kicked off her sandals and stood at the edge of the mattress. He yawned again.

'I stayed up all night. I was trying to write.'

'Did you get much done?'

'It's on the desk,' he said. 'It's shit. Don't read it.'

'Do you mind if I take a bath?' she asked.

He reached out and grabbed one of her ankles. 'Go ahead,' he said, drawing her foot to his mouth, caressing her foot.

'My feet are dirty. How can you stand it?'

'I don't care,' he said. 'It's just dirt.'

She laughed and drew her foot away. He lay smiling up into her face. 'I'm going to take a bath,' she said.

Marta sat on the edge of the bathtub watching the water run in. She was trying not to think of the spot of blood she had just found on her pants. She had washed it out quickly and hung the pants up on the towel rack and now she was trying not to think of it. Why was she bleeding? It was the wrong time. This was the second time in two weeks this had happened, and it was the wrong time. It could only mean something was wrong. 'Why am I bleeding?' she thought. 'Something is wrong.' She turned off the water and stepped into the tub. 'Think of something else,' she told herself. But she could only think of the tangle of experience that made this bleeding, these few little spots of blood, terrifying to her. She thought of the four years she had spent trying to become pregnant, of the monthly visits to the clinic where indifferent doctors had run test after test, on her and on her husband, trying to find a physical reason for her sterility. And she thought of how many times they had implied that it was all in her mind, that there was nothing wrong with her or her husband, nothing physically wrong. No reason why she could not have a child. And then she thought of her lover, whom she had taken on in a kind of frenzy of despair, three months ago. He knew nothing about those four years, nothing about her desire to have a child. He assumed that she was taking pills to avoid becoming pregnant. He knew nothing about her real reasons for coming to him, every week, and, she thought, if he suspected the truth, she had no idea how he would react. But what was the truth? Wasn't she in love with him?

'Think about something else.' And she thought about the book. She would read another story in the book and that would take her mind off the bleeding. She pulled the book out of her bag and turned to the table of contents. Here was a story entitled, 'Contraction.' She would read this story, 'Contraction.'

The bathroom door opened and Gene looked in. 'What are you doing?' he asked. 'Are you reading?' He looked disappointed.

'This book is so fascinating,' she said, looking up, ashamed. It didn't look right, she knew that, to go to one's lover and lie in the bathtub reading a book. It wasn't lover-like. And he was hurt, she could see, because she hadn't read what he had written, whatever it was, the night before, what he had left on the desk for her. She had read his work before and found it dull. He wrote about college, about his college days at a university in upstate Louisiana that was renowned for its mediocrity. He had written one novel about this undistinguished experience and now he was writing another. She closed the book. 'I'm sorry,' she said, 'It's so fascinating.'

He smiled, willingly disguising his disappointment. 'You can read it if you want,' he said. 'There's no reason why you shouldn't.'

She stood up. 'Hand me a towel,' she said.

'You can finish it if you want,' he insisted.

'No,' she laughed. 'It's foolishness. Hand me a towel.'

He held the towel out invitingly. 'I'll dry you off,' he said. 'I like to dry you off.' She stepped into his terrycloth embrace.

He dried her carefully, dropping to his knees to dry her feet and ankles. 'I didn't want to get up until you got here. I was dreaming about you.'

She leaned over him, pressing her lips against his neck. One of the women in the book, in a story she had read the day before, had left her husband and married her lover. But her husband was cruel to her, he shouted at her and made impossible demands. So it made sense that she should leave him. Marta's husband was not cruel. In fact, she thought, he was not really very different from her lover. He was less passionate. He didn't catch his breath at the thought of the insides of her knees. But he knew the insides of her knees and he knew every bit of her, as he knew himself, so why should he catch his breath?

'What is it?' Gene inquired, pausing in his progress from knee to thigh. 'What are you thinking?'

Marta met his gaze and, as always when she confronted the open affection of his face she thought, 'I'll do it. I'll break up everything, let it all go. It doesn't matter.'

'I was thinking,' she said, 'that I can't think at all when I'm with you.'

He stood up, pulling the towel up along her back, wrapping it around her shoulders. 'I wish that were true,' he said, bitterly.

While she was waiting for a streetcar to take her back uptown, Marta thought about the bleeding.

That was how it was, she thought. You started to bleed at the wrong times and then they put you in the hospital and usually they took everything out and you could never have any children. And you had to live on hormones for the rest of your life. If you didn't take the hormones you got sick and sometimes you died. So much for you. So much for your child. You lived on pills. She would tell her husband about the bleeding and he would be sympathetic and disappointed and frightened a little for her. It would be a relief to tell him. And he would say she was too young, she was only twenty-eight. She was too young. It was something temporary. She would got to the clinic and those bored doctors would look at her and give her tests and then they would say she should go into the hospital for a few days and that would be that. So much for her.

'I'll kill myself before I let them do that to me,' Marta thought. 'Or I'll just let whatever is going wrong, go wrong. I don't care if it means I bleed for the next ten years. I don't care. I'll just

let it go wrong and if it kills me then it kills me.'
This thought frightened her so badly that her
hands began to tremble. She looked at her hands,
held them up in front of her and looked at the
trembling. 'I'm so scared,' she thought. 'I've never
been this scared in my life.'

Her hands were shaking so badly that when
she tried to put her fare in the exact change
receptacle of the streetcar, the coins fell out and
clattered to the floor. The conductor frowned at
her and leaned over to pick up the coins. He had
seen her hands shaking. She put them hastily
behind her back.

'Think of him,' she thought, as she took her
seat next to an old gray-black woman who eyed
her with suspicion. 'Think of Gene.' She thought
of how he dug his fingernails into her back like
a woman, and how he had stood up, the first
time they had made love, to pull her stockings
off by the feet, shaking her out onto the sheets,
a sack of surprises, like a child, more delighted
by the unwrapping of the package than he could

ever be by anything that might be inside. What a comfort he was, she thought. 'If it weren't for him...' She felt her throat contracting around a tremendous swelling inside it, a swelling of air and saliva that would burst into a sob if her throat contracted around it one fraction of an inch tighter. It would be unbearable to break down on the streetcar, in public, to be caught crying in public. And this would be a tremendous strangling sob if it broke out, her throat quivered around it, telling her that. If it happened now, would everyone know? And how would they react? What would they do?

There was a woman crying in the story she had been reading when Gene had come into the bathroom, a woman crying in a public park. She had just begun to cry when Gene came in. She had tried not to cry, just as Marta was trying not to cry, for nearly two pages, and then, just as Gene had opened the door and said, 'What are you doing?' the woman in the story had started to cry. Marta took the book from her bag and turned to the story. There was her place. The woman saw that the man had noticed her and she was ashamed. And then the story changed its point of view and the man was noticing her, inside his own head. He saw a woman crying in a public park and he thought, 'Why is she crying?' Marta's eyes drifted across the page, to the margin, down along the side of the page, around the edge of the print. She was thinking of the pregnant woman she had seen earlier, on the streetcar, and she remembered that she had seen the woman's face, quite clearly. The woman had put her left hand over half of her face, covering one eye, and sighed a little, into the hand, her face flushing with the sigh. 'The child was moving,' Marta thought. That was what she had seen. 'The child was moving and the mother had just been thinking about her lover and then about her husband. And then the child moved and the mother thought 'Whose child is this?' She wasn't sure whose child she was carrying. It had been bothering her for some time but she hadn't wanted, really, to think about it. She tried to think of other things. She broke off with her lover and didn't tell him about the child. He didn't know she was pregnant, that she might be carrying his child, and now she had to avoid him, for if he saw her, he would know. And how would he react? What would he do, if he knew what she had done? Cheated him of his child. Cheated her husband. It was unthinkable. And then the child moved inside her. She prayed that it was her husband's. People will say, 'He looks like his father.' Except that the child was so strong within her, so insistent, so like her lover; he struck her beneath the ribs with his tiny fist, he kicked her low in the belly. 'You're a cheat,' he was saying. 'You've gone and cheated my father. Now what will you do? What will my father do without me? What will you do without my father?' And at times like that, when the child was so cruel and so insistent, she covered her face with her hand and thought, 'Whose child is this? Whose child is this?'

TRANSPOSING

A woman stands in a doorway. It is a doorway to a closet but inside is another door that leads to a cellar. The woman is standing in the closet between the two doors. She looks down at her shoes, calculating the distance between the end of her feet and the beginning of the stairs that lead to the cellar, then looks past her shoes into the dim light of the cellar. There is a sound on the stairs. A man says something to the woman. She smiles, steps back, making way for the man who is coming up out of the cellar, a tall, thin man who is pulling his long hair back into a rubber band as he speaks to her. He reaches out to her, as if to pull her into the closet with him. She laughs, backs away. The man comes out of the closet and reaches out to her again. She moves towards him. As he leans down to embrace her a few strands of his hair pull loose from the rubber band and fall across his face. The woman kisses the man's neck. She stands just outside the closet door, looking over the man's shoulder, smiling as he embraces her, as he begins to unbutton the back of her dress, smiling as she notices that she can see her own reflection in the glass cupboard that stands at the back of the closet. She smiles at her reflection as if she saw in it some intriguing secret.

So you had trouble getting used to the idea of a cellar?

I didn't know that's what it was at first. I thought the house was haunted. I thought there was something wrong with my marriage. I thought I wasn't getting enough exercise. The one afternoon I noticed I walked as far away from the cellar door as I could, and I passed it fifty times a day. It's between the kitchen and the living room. I passed it pressed against the wall. It was the cellar. The idea of a cellar. A hole under the house. There are no cellars where I come from. I didn't live in a house with a cellar until I was twenty-four.

What does the idea of a cellar mean to you?

After I left the party I went home and everyone was in bed. My husband was asleep. The children were sleeping. And I went into the bathroom, brushed my teeth, didn't think about much. Some things seemed particularly clear, almost brilliant. I sat on the edge of the tub and looked around the room. The quilted robe, in a huddle, crossing shimmering arms on the floor. The tube of toothpaste, with red lettering on the side. Its contents, visible at the tip, chalk green. How do they get it into the tube? There was my scarf hanging over a towel rack, black wool. I could see the hairs of my animals, my own hairs wound in the cloth. Short dark hairs from the dog, white hairs from the cat, thin brown hairs from my own head. And I could make out more of the hairs on the rug at my feet. I began to be disturbed by the hairs. I stood up and looked at myself in the mirror. I was thinking about the party. I was thinking about the cellar.

Was there a cellar in the house? At the party?

I'm not sure. I saw him across the room, he was leaning against a door. It could have been a cellar door. He was looking at his drink, looking at the woman who was talking to him. And it was like watching a movie as the credits go by, when it's coming into focus and the projectionist is trying to focus it, turning and trying to bring the letters into focus. And the letters blushing and blending suddenly into tight lines and the point, there's a point, when the eyes click, yes, it's clear, 'Of course. It's him.'

And as I was thinking this, he looked up at me. He looked up without meeting my eyes but he saw me there and I thought, 'He knows it. He's thinking, "Of course, it's her".'

Is that what you were thinking?

No. I didn't think that at all. I thought, 'Where are my cigarettes? Why is this woman next to me so interested in what she's saying? She's not saying anything.'

This doesn't have anything to do with the cellar.

I know. I know. I have trouble staying on the right track. My house is full of people I don't know. I don't care about them. My husband clutches me in bed, after we have said good night to them, made sure they are all settled in rooms, in beds. They are friends of friends. We settle them in for the night and then go to bed moaning to each other. 'When are they going? Where did they come from anyway?' We don't mind them that much, but we don't know them. And he clutches me to him and says, 'I love you. I love only you.' He is holding me against them in our bed, where I am alone with him and we are safe together. 'I love you. I love only you.' Passionlessly.

I think about how we bought the bed I am lying in, how we bought it together. A brass bed. It was under three layers of paint, white, green, and blue, but solid brass. We stripped it ourselves. It took a week. He did most of the work. I don't really feel that I had much to do with the acquisition. I had imagined that we would have a carved wooden bed, but I was pleased when I discovered that we had a brass bed. I didn't discover it until after we had bought it. And it took a week to strip it.

I lie in bed with my husband and I remember

how he looked at his drink. He didn't really feel right there, leaning against the door, holding a drink, talking at a party. That sort of thing embarrasses him. Then he looked at me and he was all right. He knew he was all right. I was aware of the muscles relaxing in his body. The insides of his knees, up his back, those stubborn small muscles at the base of his skull, the muscles, tenuous, incredibly delicate, that allow the eyes free movement in the sockets. I felt every one relax in him, because he had seen me. He knew I would speak to him. The place was crowded. We were suddenly, obviously alone. The woman who was talking to me looked at him, looked at me, confused.

Wasn't I listening?

My husband holds me against him, clutching me against the guests we never invited. 'I love you. I love only you.'

And I am thinking about him, looking at his drink. I don't belong in this bed. I don't belong to this man.

Do you consider yourself in love with this man?

I'm married to this man. We are married for life.

No, the other man.

My friend told me that her psychiatrist asked the same question. She was telling him about a man she is obsessed by. She was trying to describe the mechanics of her obsession. The way it repeated itself, doting on little bits of conversation, little gestures. Manifesting in things like weakened knees, little drops in the chest, as if the heart was being dislodged, making way. She tried to describe this to him, and he said, 'Do you consider yourself in love with this man?' And she told me she nodded and looked away, and said, 'Yes.'

And what did he say?

The psychiatrist? He said, 'I see.' Did it make any difference to him?

It could have.

I was sitting in a room with my students. They were all hunched over the wings of their chairs, trying to describe for me the difference between fiction and reality. They knew I didn't believe that there was any difference and so they were on the spot. One boy, a fat, sleepy, affable young man, beardless, majoring in hotel management, squinted at his page through his thick glasses, rubbed his forehead, asking himself what the difference was. He clicked the button on his pen. Down. Up. Down. Up. 'What's the difference?' he asked himself. Down. Up. What's the difference? He didn't know. He was trying hard to care. But he didn't know. He looked up at me, smiled dully at me. We both returned to our pages, wondering what the other had written.

And I was thinking that I want him to wreck his life for me.

I want you to wreck your life for me. I want you to tear everything down that you have built. Family. Friends. I want you to tell them they all must just get along without you. I want you to forget everything but me. What's the difference?

Do you consider yourself in love with this man?

I think if I could just take him through my house. Show him the rooms. 'You see this place,'

I would say. I would take him from room to room. The paintings of me. The closet full of my clothes. The desk with my papers spread all over it. the bathroom, where my scarf hangs over the towel rack. A bottle of bath oil I use from time to time, because the climate here is so hard on my skin. The kitchen, the plants hanging in the window. The glistening counter tops. The refrigerator gleaming white. The plates, white, the white light from the silverware. If I could show him this place. Show him how everything looks like someone else's idea of me. But other than that idea, no imprint of me. Nothing to do with me. It's all there. I could show him. We'd go from room to room and I would say, 'You see, you see.'

And he would know.

What is it that he would know?

Why I can't stand to see him.

The next day, after the party, I called him up and said, 'I'm not coming back there.'

First I called his secretary and she said she

would have him call. And while I was waiting —
I waited twenty minutes — I wrote over and over
on a card I had lying on my desk, a notecard, I
wrote 'I can't go back there. I can't go back there.'

I was waiting for his call. I didn't want to
interrupt him. I didn't want to inconvenience
him. But I couldn't go back there. I was deter-
mined not to do it. I knew he would call back
and talk me out of it. He's reliable. I could
depend on his call. I could depend on his talking
me out of it. I depended on that.

While I was waiting for his call I thought I
would write him a letter. Better than a call, I
would write a letter that would break his heart.
And I would send it to him at his office and it
would break his heart to think of me sitting at my
desk, in my office, which is always full of people,
writing a letter on pieces of paper I find lying
around, on the backs of assignments I've given my
students. And no one would know that I was
writing a letter, with malice, with intent to harm.

Why do you want to harm him?

I never touched him. Once, early on, his hand almost touched mine over a cigarette, and we both drew back.

You remember. And you said, 'I think you have a lot of trouble with anger.'

Was it then that you said that?

Did that surprise you? Can the answers surprise you? Can you surprise yourself? I am answering these questions to get free of you, but it isn't working. What are you trying? Is it working?

What did he say when he called back?

He said, 'This isn't a good time to think about it.'

Did you know you said that?

And I wanted to say, 'This is as good a time as we get. There's nothing to transcend here. We'll never get away from anything as long as we are trying. I know you think you can do it, but you can't lose me, you'll lose yourself. And I know you think we could reason it out, if you knew how, but you don't, and you know, if anyone knows, that I can't do it. It works pretty well to pretend you're not in your real life. I'm doing it myself. But I am in your real life and so are you. You can't hurt me, you'll hurt yourself. You can't let me go, I can't let myself go. We can't go. I win. I win.'

I wanted to say that. But I didn't say that.

What do you win?

What can I win? There's nothing to win. I see him. Time passes, then I see him again. That's my time now.

I try to determine exactly where the pain is. It's low in the stomach. It feels like a toothache. Occasionally it sends out twinges. I remember, he said, 'This isn't easy for me,' and a network, like veins, a network of pain stretches out, upward and there is a responding stab deep in the ears, a sympathetic pain that makes me clench my teeth. It only lasts a moment. It's not entirely unpleasant. An obliterating rush of pain to which I would like to succumb, but cannot. No more than I can go there and see him. No more than I can call up and say, 'Stop the pain.'

So you want to harm him?

I know I can't do that. I can't pry him loose. He's safe from me. He thinks I want him only because he's safe from me. He may be right. He won't try to find out if he's right. Because he thinks he's safe from me. But he might be wrong.

Once I told him he looked like he was waiting around for something to happen. And he said, 'So I look like I'm waiting.' He didn't much like it but he knew that it was true.

He's waiting for something to blow up, something to come apart, so that he can see it through. He knows he will be able to see it through. He is sound, like that, some people are like that. I am like that, sound at the bottom, sane and sound as rock. He relies on my sanity, I rely on his. It keeps us apart very neatly.

But he is expecting it to come apart outside him. And it's coming apart inside. Where he least expected it. He knew that it was coming apart at the party, talking to that woman, looking at his drink, looking up at me. He was wondering. 'Why can't I do this? Why is this so hard?'

And then he saw me.

And now you're waiting?

I'm waiting for the phone to ring. It rings now and then. I go to it. I can hear what he will say. He will say my name with a question. I'm ready for it. I will say. 'Yes.' I don't care much what he has in mind, what kind of arrangement he is up to or not up to. I say. 'Yes.' Every time the phone rings.

Probably for a few months. I will say, 'Yes.' And after a while I will give up and answer with my usual numbness. 'Hello?' Does someone want something of me? It that what this call is about?

How did this happen?

I am lying under my sun lamp. It's cold in my house and so I have only taken off my sweater, letting the sun lamp shine on my back and then on my chest. But I leave my jeans on, because the circle of the lamp can't reach my whole body. Only my back. Now I am lying on my stomach on the rug, under the sun lamp.

The sun lamp is a mystery to me. It puts out no heat. If it were really cold in the house I could freeze while lying under the sun lamp, because there isn't any heat. I could freeze and burn all at once, if I fell asleep under the lamp. I am careful to stay no longer than fifteen minutes. That's the most my skin can take. I have to lie under this lamp because there isn't enough sun here and my body is used to a lot of sun, a lot of heat. When I bought the lamp I imagined that it would be warm, that I would stretch out underneath its light and be warmed. How can light not be warm? How can it burn my skin, it could burn my skin black, how can it burn without warning me first?

How did you manage it? To burn with no warning?

I was freezing. It was always cold. I had to wear my coat half the time. You said when you were sick you liked the chills, you liked being cold. There's something awful about that.

I woke up last night sweating, in a fever. I had been dreaming of riding a motorcycle. There was a big mirror on the motorcycle and when I looked into it I couldn't see the traffic behind me. All I could see was my own face, my hair blown back by the speed of the motorcycle. And I knew I would lose control of the motorcycle because I couldn't stop looking at my face. My hands were very cold. I thought I was freezing, riding in a terrible cold barren place, like this place, but I woke up sweating, relieved to be sweating. I pushed the blankets away. I was so hot. I sat up in bed, pushed the blanket off my legs. My husband moaned in his sleep. I pushed the blanket off my feet. He began to turn in his sleep, to turn towards me. I put my hand on his shoulder and leaned over to kiss him and then I remembered who he was.

And I thought, 'I don't belong here.'

I am lying under the sun lamp. I have to do this, I have to make do with artificial sun, it's so humiliating. Because there isn't enough sun here.

Why is it humiliating?

It's humiliating to be told not to think about it now. That this is not a good time to think about it. Because you're not thinking clearly. You're not removed from the experience. You're still having the experience, how can you think about it? How can you think about anything else? How can you look at your drink as if you believed that cracking sound you are hearing is something that the ice cubes are doing? Why is this so hard? Why am I having so much trouble doing this?

What is that noise? Is that ice cracking? Is that what that is? Is it in my glass? Is that why it's so loud? Is it right next to me? Is that it?

A woman stands in front of a sink, washing dishes. She takes each dish from the dishpan on her right, rubs it carefully with the sponge, then rinses it beneath the running water on her left. Then she looks at the dish and deposits it in the dish rack on her right. As she allows her hand to slip under the soap suds in search of another dish, she looks out of the window over the sink. Behind her a man stands, leaning against the white counter, watching her and talking to her. Occasionally he pours water from a kettle into a coffeepot on the stove. He leans back against the counter again and watches the back of the woman.

There is a pool of expectancy around this woman. The bones in her back are straight with expectancy. Her hands, moving among the dishes, moving slowly beneath the running water, are animated by a mysterious expectancy, as if they might surprise her at any moment, as if she is not sure of her hands, of her work. She talks to the man who is pulling at a rubber band in his hair, pulling a rubber band out of his long thick hair and then stretching the rubber band, looking at it, pulling at the hair that has come loose with it. The man watches the woman nervously. There is something about her that fills him with tension. The way her hands move so steadily from left to right, the way she looks out the window each time she has finished a dish. This unnerves him. He sees that she could do this for hours with the same steady, monotonous patience, renewing each gesture, as if there were some importance to the sequence of gestures, as if washing the dishes was a ceremony, an incantation. He watches her tensely. He is entranced by her patience over this task, by the curious air of expectancy that surrounds her, by the composure with which she wipes her hands on a towel and turns towards him just as the phone rings, as if she knew, a second before the ringing began, that she would be turning in just this way, smiling at him, passing in front of him to the phone, which hangs on the wall. She picks up the receiver and turns away from him, winking at him as she turns so that he is reassured and focuses his attention on the coffeepot. And when her back is to him she looks confidently down into the mouthpiece of the phone and says, 'Yes.'

How do you feel?

I feel fine. Time doesn't mean much to me.

THE CREATOR HAS A MASTER PLAN

The last time you rejected me it was a particularly bad day. Mr. J's restaurant was out of milk and I had to do two interviews on an empty stomach. My second client had no teeth and couldn't make himself understood, he pulled at his lower lip displaying his gum line while I chewed ravenously at my pen. Eventually he made it clear that he had been living on no income at all for six months and I had to squash his doddering and insistent denials by explaining that the Department doesn't allow me to believe such stories. The rest of my clients were obstinate or desperate, my shoes were killing my feet and when I dashed in late from lunch I found my disgruntled supervisor standing by the door waiting for me. By the time I left work I had a headache and all the way home the bus window rattled. Also I found out my raise won't come through until after I go on maternity leave, and I was counting on that money.

When I saw the brown envelope sticking out of my mailbox it occurred to me that I might just leave it there until I felt better. But then I thought, maybe there'll be a note, a little encouragement. So I opened it and, as you don't recall, found the plain printed rejection slip you use, the one with the picture of the building where you work on it. It is a dull, four-story building surrounded by some northern trees I don't recognize. I looked at the picture and wondered which window is yours and if I stood under it with the rifle I spent my savings on and fired indiscriminately, would my random bullet find you as surely as yours has found me? The baby kicked furiously through this fantasy. At times we are at war with each other but in this matter we are locked in a fellowship of vengeance. Do you think your life means anything to us? Do you think we can't imagine it?

As I went upstairs I was thinking of your hair, which is undoubtedly curly, and how much I would like to pull it out in big fistfuls. Your wife never tells you how much that hair offends her, but it does. You think it is one of your finer points, in your vanity which encompasses worlds. You press your ink-stained fingers into its spongy brilliance habitually all day, a comfort to you knowing your own head is still up there, and inside your prodigious and churning brain which is beginning to tire already of these convoluted sentences, thinking the whole idea of this endeavor is misguided and such a gimmick you'd be a fool to bite.

And you're no fool. Even I who hold you in contempt know that. I don't believe it's simple-mindedness that makes you put your hand over the page and look nervously out the window of your claustrophobic office where you see — what? That young woman is not your mistress nor is that umbrella a rifle, though it could be. Your mistress is hard at her own job and couldn't get away to loiter about under windows. She doesn't even have time to think about the melancholy events of last night.

What went wrong? It wasn't anything either of you could put your finger on and say, 'That's it.

I'm through.' It's been a long time since she greeted your arrival with a particular show of enthusiasm, though of course she is always glad to see you. But you knew she was not glad to see you when you walked in. She didn't even get out of her chair. She averted her eyes from yours, turned her face away at your embrace. She is so tired of waiting on you, how many years can you keep her waiting?

After your brief and frantic coupling she threw her arm across her forehead and looked anxiously at the ceiling, as if she could find something written there; the words she needs to be free of you. Won't she look around for another lover?

No, you don't believe that. I don't know about all the time spent together, what friends you are, how you trust her, confide in her. She understands the pointless pressure you are under, the people who want to be your friend because they think you can help them, and you could. And you wouldn't mind, but. You won't remember to tell her about rejecting me.

So I take the pages out of the envelope and glancing at the top page, write the title on the bottom of the yellow slip you sent me. That goes in a folder in my file box. The pages themselves go into another envelope which I address to the people who send the slip that has a picture of a tree on it. Just a big magnolia that rejects me. Not even a building.

What I need, I conclude, is a cup of coffee, and then, perhaps, I will be ready for my dance.

I am depressed over my coffee. It is bitter, as am I. I can't help thinking of the father of my baby, I had a father for this baby, and my own rash judgment. But at least, I console myself, it was a real passion; a knockout, mind-rattling, uncontrollable passion. And it was for him, too, I knew that from the way he looked, he tilted his head and touched my chin and looked at me when he left, as if to say, who are you, what have we been doing together? It didn't last long. We were both almost ashamed of the desire we had for each other, so strong. How often does that happen? Not to you. It was not like your paltry deadening affair that's been dragging on for years. I want to be sure you know that.

We could never have lived together. He is too neat, I am messy. He is interested in his career which bores me. And then there is the small insignificant matter of his wife and two boys. Those bad boys, who, he complains, are spoiled beyond hope. They want everything, they deserve everything. I had a hunch he was serious about the need to dissolve his ties with his lazy wife who is older than me and not as good-looking. I had a miscalculation.

It's my own fault, I admit, to anyone who looks at my swollen belly as if they see there a mathematical error. I know I'm too old to be behaving like this. But I've been telling myself I would wait another year for five years and I just got tired of waiting for myself to make up my mind. I became careless, tried new methods of birth control, or none at all. I did this once before, a few years ago and nothing happened. I talk to women every day who have no husbands and no income and can't afford the babies they are always carrying, that's my job. They don't seem disturbed. There's always some way to make it.

I told myself that when the doctor came in with a long face and said, 'Well, the test is positive, I'm afraid. I'm sorry to give you such bad news.'

I burst into tears. 'How the hell do you know if it's bad news or not?' I sobbed.

'You don't seem pleased,' he observed.

I pulled myself together, rubbed my eyes with the backs of my hands. 'What do you suggest?'

'It's early yet. We can schedule you into the hospital next week.'

'I thought it took nine months.'

'I assumed you didn't want to have the child.'

I fumbled through my bag for the keys to the car I borrowed for this occasion. 'Of course you did, you bastard,' I mumbled. 'Which is why you won't see me again.' And I left.

My lover, I thought, as I fought a wave of nausea in the parking lot, will understand.

Which he did, really, better than I wanted him to. His face literally went grey when I told him. 'We'll have to find an abortionist,' says he gently to the distraught woman beside him on the bed. A woman he doesn't really know well enough or he never would have said that. 'How could you let this happen?'

Yes, I did scream and showed bad form, the kind his wife has not the energy to show. 'Why not just kill me and solve all your problems all at once? I am liable to become a serious inconvenience very shortly.'

'You can do what you want,' he assured me. 'But the trouble is I don't have much money. I can raise maybe $500. Will that help?'

'I don't want your money,' I said. Five hundred dollars was more than I expected. How could he write off $500 without his wife knowing?

'I feel responsible,' he explained.

'Crummy feeling, isn't it?'

'I can't say I like it.'

'It doesn't matter. I don't hold you to it.'

'It just never occurred to me that you wouldn't be taking some precautions,' he accused.

I decided to be as honest as possible. 'You're sure you don't want to leave your wife. I mean, this is as good an excuse as you'll ever get. And I'll take care of your boys. We wouldn't have to marry, we could just see how it goes. I'd keep working for a while.'

He smiled wearily. 'There's no chance of that. Even if I hated her, I wouldn't do that.'

I said, 'Oh.'

Later I said, 'Look, it will just be grief to see you and I'm going to have a lot on my mind so let's not continue this thing.'

'You don't want to see me?' His relief showed.

'No. I'd rather not.'

Three days later I got a check for $500. I thought I would send it back but I left it on the kitchen table for a few days and then I got the new doctor's bill. I put the check in my savings account. At the same time I opened another savings account and put $50 in it. I did not, at that time, know what this account was for.

I have that savings book in front of me as I drink my coffee, and I look at the line of zeros at the bottom of the page. The rifle that caused those zeros is leaning against a twenty-five-pound box of Milkbones in the pantry behind me. I am nearly ready for my dance.

I am unconsciously unbuttoning the buttons on my huge navy maternity blouse. In the last two months I have taken advantage of every opportunity to be without clothes; the touch of material makes my skin ache. When I am naked I look funny but it doesn't bother me and there is no on else to see. I remember that when I read about Sharon Tate's murder it struck me as odd, indecent, that she had been killed in bikini pajamas. A pregnant beauty in bikini pajamas, it was almost just. And the article suggested that this was what she always wore. At that time I didn't understand, thought her choice of apparel somewhat obscene, but now, as I pull off my unbearable underclothes and spread a towel on my wooden chair so it wouldn't be as hard on my bare rear, I think she must have been like me. Things were going well, the baby was strong inside, she could feel that, but her skin hurt and it was always hot. Better to wear as little as possible, or nothing at all. Just waiting, in that petulant, half-humorous way all pregnant women must wait out the last month or so, fanning themselves, feeling oppressed and incredibly lonely, complaining about their feet, waiting with a dull anxiety like a heart-throb.

I have no reason to dread the unthinkable fate she had not the foreknowledge to fear, but I don't mean to suggest at any point that I am not afraid. It comes mostly at night, when I am torn out of sleep by insistent, violent movement inside. It feels like the baby senses something going drastically wrong, wants to wake me to it, wake me as fast as possible. I turn on my back in a panic, reach out over my head and grasp the bars at the end of the bed for an anchor. Because

I am floating away, floating in space, struggling hopelessly. Inside me there is an inexplicable terror. I ask myself, who feels me inside, thrashing about in the darkness, in whose deep sleeping interior am I the fear?

This fear is never far from me. I sit with it, large, unsightly, naked, at my table recalling what I had forgotten, that the day I mailed that manuscript to you was the same day I bought the rifle.

After I went to the post office I walked down Royal, looking at the fine and less than fine antiques in the windows. The coin-shop window was so dark and dusty that I stood looking in the glass for a few moments before I realized what they had to sell. There was a tray of coins in the front of the case, behind that two matched pistols with carved handles and behind these, on a free-standing rack, three highly polished rifles. I went inside. The walls were covered with rifles, of every possible description. I glanced at the price tags: $450, $700, $250, nothing I could afford. A man came from the back of the store and asked if he could help me. I looked at him carefully. I have started looking at everyone carefully – will my child turn out like that? This man was prematurely bald, a few strands of thin blond hair grew from the crown of his head and had been allowed to touch the back of his neck in a travesty of youth. His eyes were pale, blue, fishy, his skin pale and without character, his mouth narrow and barely darker than the rest of his face. His nose was a surprise: long, narrow, a fine aristocratic bridge, nostrils flared delicately, a nose women would envy. His expression was nervous but friendly. I gestured vaguely to the rifles. 'Do these all work?'

'Some do,' he said. 'We don't sell them to work. They're antiques. They haven't been test-fired. But some should work. I can generally tell, if there's a spring missing or something. I'll tell you, "There's a spring missing," or whatever is missing, or that it should work if nothing's missing, though that doesn't mean it will work.'

I leaned against the counter, looking at all the rifles for one that would catch me, hold me, one that was particularly fine. 'They're beautiful.' I said.

The man smiled, relaxed. He would gladly stand and admire his rifles with me all afternoon if I liked. 'How much is that one – third from the top?' I asked.

He turned to a book on the counter and flipped through the pages. 'That's a Winchester. It's $350.'

'Does it fire a bullet?'

'No. It takes a powder charge.'

'Loose gunpowder?'

'Yes. You have to pack it in. That one was made in 1840.'

'Do you have any that fire bullets?'

'A cartridge? Yes, these over here.' He pointed to the wall behind us. 'These are all cartridge rifles.'

'Do they cost as much?'

'Well, they vary,' he said. He consulted his book. 'The one on the top there, number 17, that's $400. Under that 18 is $200, 19 is $175, and 20 is $350.'

'That third one there is $175?' I asked. It was the one I liked best. I never choose the cheapest item in any selection. It seemed important that I look at this anomaly.

'Yes. That's a Colt Lightning. It's a good rifle. Fires a cartridge. You load it from the side. You see that wooden piece on the barrel? You pull that forward, then back to advance the cartridge.'

'I've seen people do that on television.'

'Yes,' he agreed. 'That one was made in 1875. That would be a rifle a hunting man would use.'

'What would it kill?'

He smiled a yellow toothed smile. Wasn't I charmingly frank? 'Oh, you could kill a deer with it. A small bear.'

'From what distance?'

Another nervous smile. '150 yards.'

'Could I hold it?'

He gave me a curious look. 'Sure,' he said. 'I'll get it down.'

While he was pulling out his stepladder and unlocking the rifle from its rack I had a brief fantasy. Lately I've been plagued by roaches, not the little kind that live in the kitchen, but big outdoor roaches that come in the bathroom window and fly into my face when I'm brushing my teeth. Horrible creatures. I keep a spray and a shoe around to kill them with but I'm not fast enough. They get away, sneak back through cracks in the walls, prepare their next attack. I pictured myself lying on my back in a tub of warm water, my rifle propped across the edge of the tub, just touching my big belly. A roach jumps in the window, scrambles down the wall in my direction. I slide smoothly down under my weapon, take quick aim and a second later the wretched creature has been blown out of existence. A hole in the bathroom wall and not a trace of my oppressor, not even one flimsy writhing little leg.

In a moment the man had returned from his perch on his stepladder and the rifle was in my hands. 'It's not as heavy as I thought it would be,' I said.

'No, it's not a heavy gun. They make them a lot lighter now, though. A new rifle, some of those are really light. That rifle Lee Harvey Oswald used, now that was much lighter than this one.

And of course, more streamlined. It was specially made. Weapons today are more practical.'

'But not as beautiful.' I ran my hand down the long, cool steel of the barrel, then examined the oily smooth wood of the stock. 'Does it come apart?'

'Sure. You can break it down.'

'Show me how to load it.'

'You put the cartridge back in here, like this.' He pushed the pump forward, pointing out a long rod just beneath it. 'Then pull it back –' The mechanism clicked into place.

I held the rifle again and examined it. I know what you think I was thinking and what the allure was and all that, and I don't deny it. But I felt something else as well, something that was not purely sexual, but more primitive still. I felt I would require it for survival.

'You'd have to have it test-fired and checked out. It might need something but as far as I know it should work. The cartridges would be hard to get.' He paused. 'Most people don't want these for shooting. They're antiques.'

'Yes,' I agreed. 'Well, I wouldn't want it for shooting. I don't know how.'

It took me awhile to talk him down to $150. Towards the end another man, a fat swarthy man with a mustache, came out from the back room and joined in the discussion. He seemed to think I should have the rifle and it was he who finally said $150 would be acceptable. I wrote a check that would bounce if I didn't go straight to the bank. Then I had to fill out a registration form, purely a formality I was assured, and it was mine. Wrapped in brown paper. I walked along the street with the package resting across my shoulder like a pioneer stalking through the wilderness. What did people think? What baby product would look just like a rifle in a package? I wished them all luck with their guessing.

Now my rifle leans against the box of Milkbones in the pantry. I see it twenty times a day. I am aware of it in the evenings when it is warm and I sit in my armchair and fan myself aimlessly, staring into space, drinking iced tea, examining my breasts to see if they are sagging yet, my calves for varicose veins, my big stomach for places where stretch marks might be. So far, so good. I'm holding up pretty well. I'm thankful for the warm climate and the humidity which keeps my skin from becoming brittle. When I feel cool I put on my Pharaoh Sanders record and begin my secret dance.

At first my dance is shy, slow, mostly arm waving and hip swaying, but as the music grows more intense so does my abandon and my dance becomes a contest. I stretch all the muscles that are so recalcitrant, stand up on the tips of my aching feet so that the arches pop, bend backward as far as my back will let me (surprisingly far for my big stomach, I can nearly touch the floor behind me) twist at what's left of my waist, even flex every joint in my swollen fingers. If anyone saw this dance, I imagine it would strike them blind, deaf and dumb. The baby kicks hard throughout, harder and harder, a clear demand, dance more, dance harder. It doesn't matter if I am drenched with sweat, when I whirl around drops of moisture fly from my fingertips. You wouldn't think a pregnant woman would have the stamina to dance so wildly and so long. I imagine myself on a beach somewhere, dancing to the chagrin of the ocean, in some wood clearing, the deer run like hell, or on your desk top and your papers are flying away beneath my feet and all your thoughts are scattering. Can a pregnant woman dance like this, burning all my thoughts away? I would burn up your office, my friend, when we meet, I would burn up your world. You would be calling your wife on one phone and your mistress on the other, 'Help me, I'm lost, I'm lost.' And then I would dance out the door and down the hall, past your colleagues' offices, down the stairs and out under those peculiar trees, leaving you huddled in a corner, your head buried in your arms and your eyes on fire.

After my dance I am exhausted and usually fall on the floor next to the dog, who eyes me dubiously. It takes me awhile to get my breath back. Every night I tell myself it is pointless to get up and do what I will do next, and every night, in spite of myself, I do it. I got back to the kitchen and take out my checkbook and my savings account. I've gone over it again and again, I am $600 short of being able to live until I go back to work. How can this be? And this is a rough estimate, if I don't waste another cent until the baby is born, if I pay the hospital in the smallest possible allotments, if there are not complications. Six hundred dollars short. I don't know where I'm going to get the money. I look at the figures and add them up again. I have never run across a fact that held less reality for me. I know the day will come when I will go to the bank and there will be nothing to draw out, but I can't believe in that day. Something will break. Something will have to come through. I rub my big belly with the palm of my hand and my child is frighteningly still. Think of something, I tell myself. Try to think of something.

Perhaps I think of you when I take the rifle

out of the pantry and prop it across my knees. Of you and your mistress and of something else you would like to forget, the time you were looking for a match at her apartment. She went out to the drugstore because she had such a headache and not an aspirin in the place. And then you had to have a cigarette. That was simple enough, a craving for tobacco. Surely there was a match in the kitchen. You didn't feel self-conscious about going through the drawers in the kitchen, where you found evidence of extreme organization: large pots in one cabinet, small ones in another, lids all in one drawer neatly arranged, but no matches. The stove was no help, electric. Perhaps you felt a little nervous when you went through her desk, because there were letters bound with rubber bands and it was hard not to look at the return addresses. You picked up a stack from a certain Southern city, a name you would not recognize though you've seen it before. You found paper clips, staples, sharpened pencils, even a box of paper hole reinforcements, but no matches. The bathroom cabinets held neither surprises nor matches. Your search of her bedroom was casual, scan the tops of the dresser and chest of drawers, a quick glance at the contents of the nightstand. Then the dresser drawers, sweaters neatly folded in the top drawer, short pants and pullover shirts in the next, and in the third, lingerie. What made you pause over the contents of this drawer; will you ever guess? Surely you didn't expect to find matches among those delicate laces and nylons? Were you simply attracted to the softness of the stuff, the pastel colors, the light perfume that rose enticingly when you opened the drawer? You pressed your palm against the bodice of a blue embroidered gown and felt something surprisingly cool and hard through the cloth You slipped your hand beneath the gown and closed your trespassing fingers on a blade as sharp as a razor. A razor? A knife? You had only seen one other like it in your life, a hunting knife a friend once showed you, very expensive, perfectly weighted, with a blade that could skin a deer (or an enemy, you thought then) in a matter of minutes. Why would a woman buy such a knife, and why keep it here, hidden beneath her most feminine and intimate apparel? You experienced a chill that made you step back, holding the knife out before your astounded eyes, even as you heard her key turning in the lock of the living room door.

I can see you standing there as I open my linseed oil and press a cloth against the lip of the bottle. I use three kinds of oil on my rifle: one for the stock, one for the barrel and one for the rod inside the pump. Yesterday I looked in the phone book and found a number for a man who will test-fire it and show me how to use it. I haven't called him yet. For the present it clears my head to oil and clean the rifle carefully, to feel its reassuring weight across my big stomach, to sit sweating and naked at my kitchen table, a drop of oil shimmering just above my protruding navel, rubbing and polishing this useless weapon until it gleams.